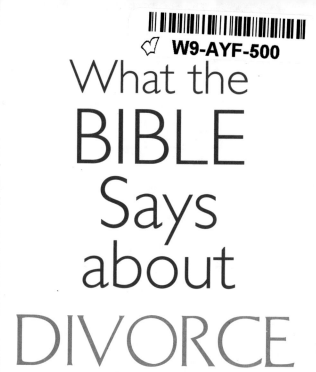

What the
BIBLE
Says
about
DIVORCE

What the
BIBLE
Says
about
DIVORCE

BARBOUR
PUBLISHING

Published by Barbour Publishing, Inc., P.O. Box 719, Uhrichsville, Ohio 44683, www.barbourbooks.com

Our mission is to publish and distribute inspirational products offering exceptional value and biblical encouragement to the masses.

 Member of the
Evangelical Christian
Publishers Association

Printed in the United States of America

CONTENTS

INTRODUCTION
WHY IS THIS HAPPENING TO ME?

Many counselors believe that divorce is one of the most painful events that can happen to a person. Because of the prolonged fights, hurts, and feelings of rejection, some divorced individuals can take longer to heal than other people whose spouses die unexpectedly.

If the logistics of divorce weren't hard enough, the feelings that accompany them can make life feel unbearable. But even in the worst of times, you're not alone. God has not abandoned you during this difficult time. And while His presence is near, His comforting words can provide much of the healing and direction you need.

Enclosed in this book are carefully chosen
words of God for you during this difficult time.
They're accompanied by the words of men
and women who have experienced many
of the same things you're experiencing.
You'll also find some practical thoughts to
help you take some next, healthy steps.
While today may not be easy, you don't have
to take the steps alone. Find hope as you enjoy
taking God's hand through the days ahead.

CHAPTER 1

CAN THESE HURTS BE HEALED?

The tears come so quickly. When I got married, I never imagined that all our dreams could shatter into pieces like this. I feel like a complete failure—rejected and alone. I'm so hurt and depressed, and I don't see myself ever getting past this. To be honest, it's hard to find much reason to get out of bed in the morning. It just hurts too badly to face the future.

■ Alissa, age 27, Rhode Island ■

FEELING
LIKE A FAILURE

My flesh and my heart fail;
But God is the strength of my heart and
my portion forever.

PSALM 73:26 NKJV

I to him who is able to keep you from
stumbling and to present you blameless
before the presence of his glory with great
joy, to the only God, our Savior, through Jesus
Christ our Lord, be glory, majesty, dominion,
and authority, before all time and now and
forever. Amen.

JUDE 1:24–25 ESV

■ "The LORD will fight for you; you need only
   to be still."

EXODUS 14:14 NIV

■ I will be glad and rejoice in your unfailing love,
   for you have seen my troubles,
   and you care about the anguish of
   my soul.

PSALM 31:7 NLT

■ We are afflicted in every way, but not
crushed; perplexed, but not driven to despair;
persecuted, but not forsaken; struck down,
but not destroyed; always carrying in the
body the death of Jesus, so that the life of
Jesus may also be manifested in our bodies.

2 CORINTHIANS 4:8–10 ESV

FEELING CRUSHED

■ The LORD is close to the brokenhearted;
he rescues those whose spirits are
crushed.

PSALM 34:18 NLT

■ Trust in him at all times, O people;
pour out your hearts to him,
for God is our refuge.

PSALM 62:8 NIV

■ God cares for you, so turn all your worries
over to him.

1 PETER 5:7 CEV

"Don't be afraid, I've redeemed you.
I've called your name. You're mine.
When you're in over your head, I'll be there
    with you.
When you're in rough waters, you will not
    go down.
When you're between a rock and a hard
    place, it won't be a dead end—
Because I am God, your personal God,
    The Holy of Israel, your Savior.
I paid a huge price for you:
    all of Egypt, with rich Cush and Seba
    thrown in!
That's how much you mean to me!
    That's how much I love you!
I'd sell off the whole world to get you back,
    trade the creation just for you."

ISAIAH 43:1–4 MSG

Praise the LORD, O my soul;
all my inmost being, praise his holy name.
Praise the LORD, O my soul,
and forget not all his benefits—
who forgives all your sins
and heals all your diseases,
who redeems your life from the pit
and crowns you with love and
compassion.

PSALM 103:1–4 NIV

The LORD God is waiting
to show how kind he is
and to have pity on you.
The LORD always does right;
he blesses those who trust him.

ISAIAH 30:18 CEV

■ What, then, shall we say in response to this?
If God is for us, who can be against us? He
who did not spare his own Son, but gave him
up for us all—how will he not also, along with
him, graciously give us all things? Who will
bring any charge against those whom God
has chosen? It is God who justifies. Who is
he that condemns? Christ Jesus, who died—
more than that, who was raised to life—is at
the right hand of God and is also interceding
for us. Who shall separate us from the
love of Christ? Shall trouble or hardship
or persecution or famine or nakedness or
danger or sword? As it is written:

> "For your sake we face death all day long;
> we are considered as sheep to be
> slaughtered."

No, in all these things we are more than
conquerors through him who loved us.

ROMANS 8:31'–37 NIV

FEELING REJECTED

■ Since God assured us, "I'll never let you down,
>   never walk off and leave you,"
>   we can boldly quote,
> God is there, ready to help;
> I'm fearless no matter what.
> Who or what can get to me?

HEBREWS 13:5 MSG

■ For this is what the LORD says. . .
> "As a mother comforts her child,
>   so will I comfort you. . . ."
> When you see this, your heart will rejoice
>   and you will flourish like grass;
>   the hand of the LORD will be made
>   known to his servants,
>   but his fury will be shown to his foes.

ISAIAH 66:12–14 NIV

The LORD is my shepherd, I shall not be
in want.
He makes me lie down in green pastures,
he leads me beside quiet waters,
he restores my soul.
He guides me in paths of righteousness
for his name's sake.

PSALM 23:1–3 NIV

"Do not let your hearts be troubled. Trust in
God; trust also in me. In my Father's house
are many rooms; if it were not so, I would
have told you. I am going there to prepare a
place for you. And if I go and prepare a place
for you, I will come back and take you to be
with me that you also may be where I am.
You know the way to the place where I
am going."

JOHN 14:1–4 NIV

But Zion said, "I don't get it. God has left me.
My Master has forgotten I even exist."
"Can a mother forget the infant at her breast,
walk away from the baby she bore?
But even if mothers forget,
I'd never forget you—never.
Look, I've written your names on the backs of
    my hands.
The walls you're rebuilding are never out of
    my sight.
Your builders are faster than your wreckers.
The demolition crews are gone for good.
Look up, look around, look well!
See them all gathering, coming to you?"

ISAIAH 49:14–16 MSG

FINDING HEALING

■ "I will give you back your health
and heal your wounds," says the LORD.

JEREMIAH 30:17 NLT

■ Therefore we do not lose heart.
Though outwardly we are wasting away,
yet inwardly we are being renewed
day by day.

2 CORINTHIANS 4:16 NIV

■ "Blessed are you who are poor, for yours
is the kingdom of God.
Blessed are you who are hungry now,
for you shall be satisfied.
Blessed are you who weep now,
for you shall laugh."

LUKE 6:20–21 ESV

21

■ Beloved, do not be surprised at the fiery
trial when it comes upon you to test you,
as though something strange were hap-
pening to you. But rejoice insofar as you
share Christ's sufferings, that you may also
rejoice and be glad when his glory
is revealed.

1 PETER 4:12–13 ESV

■ Heal me, O LORD, and I shall be healed;
Save me, and I shall be saved,
For You are my praise.

JEREMIAH 17:14 NKJV

■ O Lord my God, I cried to you for help,
and you have healed me.

PSALM 30:2 NRSV

■ "I will heal my people and will let them enjoy
abundant peace and security."

JEREMIAH 33:6 NIV

23

RESTORING THE BROKEN

He heals the brokenhearted
and binds up their wounds.

PSALM 147:3 NIV

May our Lord Jesus Christ himself and God
our Father, who loved us and by his grace
gave us eternal encouragement and good
hope, encourage your hearts and strengthen
you in every good deed and word.

2 THESSALONIANS 2:16–17 NIV

So if Christ keeps giving me his power, I will
gladly brag about how weak I am. Yes, I am
glad to be weak or insulted or mistreated
or to have troubles and sufferings, if it is for
Christ. Because when I am weak, I am strong.

2 CORINTHIANS 12:9–10 CEV

■ Be strong and take heart,
    all you who hope in the LORD.

PSALM 31:24 NIV

■ He personally carried our sins
    in his body on the cross
so that we can be dead to sin
    and live for what is right.
By his wounds
    you are healed.

1 PETER 2:24 NLT

■ "The thief comes only to steal and kill and
destroy; I have come that they may have life,
and have it to the full."

JOHN 10:10 NIV

■ The Spirit of God, who raised Jesus from
the dead, lives in you. And just as God raised
Christ Jesus from the dead, he will give life to
your mortal bodies by this same Spirit living
within you.

ROMANS 8:11 NLT

OVERCOMING AN ABUSIVE PAST

■ "You're blessed when you feel you've lost what is most dear to you. Only then can you be embraced by the One most dear to you."

MATTHEW 5:4 MSG

■ Yet what we suffer now is nothing compared to the glory he will reveal to us later.

ROMANS 8:18 NLT

■ On that day you will be glad, even if you have to go through many hard trials for a while. Your faith will be like gold that has been tested in a fire. And these trials will prove that your faith is worth much more than gold that can be destroyed. They will show that you will be given praise and honor and

27

glory when Jesus Christ returns. You have never seen Jesus, and you don't see him now. But still you love him and have faith in him, and no words can tell how glad and happy you are to be saved. That's why you have faith.

1 PETER 1:6–9 CEV

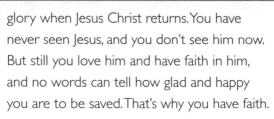

As he passed by, he saw a man blind from birth. And his disciples asked him, "Rabbi, who sinned, this man or his parents, that he was born blind?"

Jesus answered, "It was not that this man sinned, or his parents, but that the works of God might be displayed in him."

JOHN 9:1–3 ESV

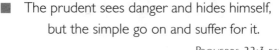

The prudent sees danger and hides himself,
but the simple go on and suffer for it.

PROVERBS 22:3 ESV

For God gave us a spirit not of fear but of
power and love and self-control.

2 TIMOTHY 1:7 ESV

ONE MOMENT
AT A TIME

HEALING
THE HURTS

1. Grieve the loss. Divorce is always a loss. While every situation is unique, feelings of anger, guilt, insecurity, and sadness are normal. It's important to work through each emotion and understand what you're feeling so that you can find the closure you need.

2. Accept the change. While divorce may not be your first choice, it's likely to be a defining moment in your life. While there are surely lessons to learn from the past, there is no benefit in dwelling on past hurts or failures. Yes, life is different now. No, don't wallow over what's happened. Though life

will never be the same as it was, your future still holds hope.

3. Get supportive help. Don't walk through these days alone. Connect with a counselor, a pastor, or a mature friend. Supportive help during this time can help you implement life changes, keep a positive outlook, and maintain personal growth.

4. Work at moving on. Choose to make this change good for you. Find ways to embrace your new life. Each day, make it a point to find at least one thing to praise and thank God for.

CHAPTER 2

WHAT DOES GOD THINK OF ME NOW?

When I'm at church, I look around at the other
people sitting comfortably in their pews.
They've got their acts together and are successful
in their lives and marriages. Me? I'm the newly
divorced guy—apparently inept at marriage.
It's hard not to sit there and feel like a complete
failure. But then I remember God's love and
I realize that He did not save me from my sins
so that I'd feel this way. Not at all. The fact is,
I'm forgiven. And no one in this building has
experienced His love more than I.

■ Jonathan, age 34, Pennsylvania ■

KNOWING YOUR IDENTITY IN CHRIST

■ But to all who did receive him, who believed in his name, he gave the right to become children of God.

JOHN 1:12 ESV

■ For you are all children of God through faith in Christ Jesus.

GALATIANS 3:26 NLT

■ For all who are led by the Spirit of God are children of God.
So you have not received a spirit that makes you fearful slaves. Instead, you received God's Spirit when he adopted you as his own children. Now we call him, "Abba, Father."

ROMANS 8:14–15 NLT

■ "I no longer call you servants, because a servant does not know his master's business. Instead, I have called you friends, for everything that I learned from my Father I have made known to you."

JOHN 15:15 NIV

■ All this is from God, who reconciled us to himself through Christ and gave us the ministry of reconciliation: that God was reconciling the world to himself in Christ, not counting men's sins against them. And he has committed to us the message of reconciliation. We are therefore Christ's ambassadors, as though God were making his appeal through us. We implore you on Christ's behalf: Be reconciled to God. God made him who had no sin to be sin for us, so that in him we might become the righteousness of God.

2 CORINTHIANS 5:18–21 NIV

■ Praise the God and Father of our Lord Jesus Christ for the spiritual blessings that Christ has brought us from heaven! Before the world was created, God had Christ choose us to live with him and to be his holy and innocent and loving people. God was kind and decided that Christ would choose us to be God's own adopted children. God was very kind to us because of the Son he dearly loves, and so we should praise God.

EPHESIANS 1:3–6 CEV

■ Therefore, since we have been made right in God's sight by faith, we have peace with God because of what Jesus Christ our Lord has done for us.

ROMANS 5:1 NLT

■ "For the LORD will not forsake His people, for His great name's sake, because it has pleased the LORD to make you His people."

1 SAMUEL 12:22 NKJV

■ Know that the LORD, He is God;
It is He who has made us, and not we
    ourselves;
We are His people and the sheep of His
    pasture.

PSALM 100:3 NKJV

BELIEVING IN GOD'S FORGIVENESS

■ My dear children, I am writing this to you so that you will not sin. But if anyone does sin, we have an advocate who pleads our case before the Father. He is Jesus Christ, the one who is truly righteous.

1 JOHN 2:1 NLT

■ If we confess our sins, he is faithful and just and will forgive us our sins and purify us from all unrighteousness.

1 JOHN 1:9 NIV

■ So whenever we are in need, we should come bravely before the throne of our merciful God. There we will be treated with undeserved kindness, and we will find help.

HEBREWS 4:16 CEV

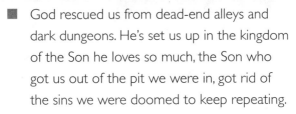

God rescued us from dead-end alleys and dark dungeons. He's set us up in the kingdom of the Son he loves so much, the Son who got us out of the pit we were in, got rid of the sins we were doomed to keep repeating.

COLOSSIANS 1:13–14 MSG

But you, O Lord, are a compassionate and
    gracious God,
slow to anger, abounding in love and
    faithfulness.

PSALM 86:15 NIV

Help us, O God of our salvation!
    Help us for the glory of your name.
Save us and forgive our sins
    for the honor of your name.

PSALM 79:9 NLT

■ In him we have redemption through his
blood, the forgiveness of sins, in accordance
with the riches of God's grace that
he lavished on us with all wisdom and
understanding.

EPHESIANS 1:7–8 NIV

■ "Come now, let's settle this," says the LORD.
"Though your sins are like scarlet, I will make
them as white as snow. Though they are red
like crimson, I will make them as white as
wool."

ISAIAH 1:18 NLT

■ "I—yes, I alone—will blot out your sins for
my own sake and will never think of them
again."

ISAIAH 43:25 NLT

SENSING GOD'S LOVE

■ But the LORD watches over those who fear him, those who rely on his unfailing love.

PSALM 33:18 NLT

■ For God so loved the world, that he gave his only Son, that whoever believes in him should not perish but have eternal life.

JOHN 3:16 ESV

■ But God demonstrates his own love for us in this: While we were still sinners, Christ died for us.

ROMANS 5:8 NIV

■ Great is his faithfulness; his mercies begin afresh each morning. I say to myself, "The LORD is my inheritance; therefore, I will hope in him!"

LAMENTATIONS 3:23–24 NLT

■ We know what real love is because Jesus gave up his life for us.

1 JOHN 3:16 NLT

■ The Lord isn't slow about keeping his promises, as some people think he is. In fact, God is patient, because he wants everyone to turn from sin and no one to be lost.

2 PETER 3:9 CEV

■ The LORD is good,

   a refuge in times of trouble.

He cares for those who trust in him.

NAHUM 1:7 NIV

■ But God put his love on the line for us by offering his Son in sacrificial death while we were of no use whatever to him.

ROMANS 5:8 MSG

■ He found them in a desert land,

   in an empty, howling wasteland.

He surrounded them and watched over

   them; he guarded them as he would

   guard his own eyes.

DEUTERONOMY 32:10 NLT

■ For I am convinced that neither death nor
life, neither angels nor demons, neither the
present nor the future, nor any powers,
neither height nor depth, nor anything else in
all creation, will be able to separate us from
the love of God that is in Christ Jesus our
Lord.

ROMANS 8:38–39 NIV

AVOIDING SELF-PITY AND SHAME

■ As the Scripture says, "Anyone who trusts in him will never be put to shame."

ROMANS 10:11 NIV

■ He has never let you down,
   never looked the other way
   when you were being kicked around.
He has never wandered off to do his own
   thing; he has been right there, listening.

PSALM 22:24 MSG

■ From the ends of the earth I call to you,
   I call as my heart grows faint;
   lead me to the rock that is higher than I.
For you have been my refuge,
   a strong tower against the foe.

PSALM 61:2–3 NIV

45

■ "Do not be afraid; you will not suffer shame.
Do not fear disgrace; you will not be
　　humiliated.
You will forget the shame of your youth
　　and remember no more the reproach
　　of your widowhood."

ISAIAH 54:4 NIV

■ In you, O LORD, do I take refuge;
　　let me never be put to shame!

PSALM 71:1 ESV

■ That is why I am suffering as I am. Yet I am
not ashamed, because I know whom I have
believed, and am convinced that he is able
to guard what I have entrusted to him for
that day.

2 TIMOTHY 1:12 NIV

■ Humble yourselves, therefore, under God's mighty hand, that he may lift you up in due time.

1 PETER 5:6 NIV

■ He will wipe all tears from their eyes, and there will be no more death, suffering, crying, or pain. These things of the past are gone forever.

REVELATION 21:4 CEV

■ So now there is no condemnation for those who belong to Christ Jesus.

ROMANS 8:1 NLT

■ A happy heart makes the face cheerful, but heartache crushes the spirit.

PROVERBS 15:13 NIV

47

■ But as for me, it is good to be near God.
I have made the Sovereign LORD my refuge;
     I will tell of all your deeds.

PSALM 73:28 NIV

■ Don't be like the people of this world, but let
God change the way you think. Then you will
know how to do everything that is good and
pleasing to him.

ROMANS 12:2 CEV

■ For our light and momentary troubles are
achieving for us an eternal glory that far
outweighs them all.

2 CORINTHIANS 4:17 NIV

This then is how we know that we belong to the truth, and how we set our hearts at rest in his presence whenever our hearts condemn us. For God is greater than our hearts, and he knows everything.

1 JOHN 3:19–20 NIV

Let us fix our eyes on Jesus, the author and perfecter of our faith, who for the joy set before him endured the cross, scorning its shame, and sat down at the right hand of the throne of God. Consider him who endured such opposition from sinful men, so that you will not grow weary and lose heart.

HEBREWS 12:2–3 NIV

ONE MOMENT
AT A TIME

REINFORCING
GOD'S TRUTH

1. Reflect on God's forgiveness. Reread the section that tells about God's forgiveness and bolster your belief that God's forgiveness is not conditional.

2. Identify where you find your worth. Some people find their value in being a spouse or a parent. Others find it in their career or in their role at church. God wants you to find your identity as His child.

3. Remember that Jesus can never love you more or less than He loves you right now. As His child, you have God's constant love.

No trouble, divorce, or sin can ever diminish His love for you.

4. God does not grow angry or ashamed of His children. Self-pity and shame are natural human emotions, but they're not ones you should dwell on. God forgives and empowers. And when He moves on, so should you.

CHAPTER 3

AM I WRONG TO FEEL THIS WAY?

Sometimes I hang up the phone after talking
with my ex and I just want to scream.
Nothing makes my blood pressure soar as much
as when someone merely mentions his name.
I know I need to get past this,
but the anger won't go away.

■ LaDawn, age 44, Oregon ■

FACING YOUR ANGER

■ "In your anger do not sin: Do not let the sun go down while you are still angry."

EPHESIANS 4:26 NIV

■ Be patient and trust the LORD. Don't let it bother you when all goes well for those who do sinful things.
Don't be angry or furious. Anger can lead to sin.

PSALM 37:7–8 CEV

■ Human anger does not produce the righteousness God desires.

JAMES 1:20 NLT

■ But now you must stop doing such things. You must quit being angry, hateful, and evil. You must no longer say insulting or cruel things about others.

COLOSSIANS 3:8 CEV

■ Don't be quick to fly off the handle. Anger boomerangs. You can spot a fool by the lumps on his head.

ECCLESIASTES 7:9 MSG

■ Don't befriend angry people or associate with hot-tempered people, or you will learn to be like them and endanger your soul.

PROVERBS 22:24–25 NLT

■ Beloved, never avenge yourselves, but leave it to the wrath of God, for it is written, "Vengeance is mine, I will repay, says the Lord." To the contrary, "if your enemy is hungry, feed him; if he is thirsty, give him something to drink; for by so doing you will heap burning coals on his head." Do not be overcome by evil, but overcome evil with good.

ROMANS 12:19–21 ESV

■ "I'm telling you that anyone who is so much as angry with a brother or sister is guilty of murder. Carelessly call a brother 'idiot!' and you just might find yourself hauled into court. Thoughtlessly yell 'stupid!' at a sister and you are on the brink of hellfire. The simple moral fact is that words kill.

MATTHEW 5:22 MSG

If you see your enemy hungry, go buy him
lunch; if he's thirsty, bring him a drink.
Your generosity will surprise him with
goodness, and GOD will look after you.

PROVERBS 25:21–22 MSG

FINDING GOD'S GRACE

■ "But in your great mercy you did not put an end to them or abandon them, for you are a gracious and merciful God."

NEHEMIAH 9:31 NIV

■ You surely don't think much of God's wonderful goodness or of his patience and willingness to put up with you. Don't you know that the reason God is good to you is because he wants you to turn to him?

ROMANS 2:4 CEV

■ For it is by grace you have been saved, through faith—and this not from yourselves, it is the gift of God—not by works, so that no one can boast.

EPHESIANS 2:8–9 NIV

"You have granted me life and steadfast love, and your care has preserved my spirit."

JOB 10:12 ESV

I always thank God for you because of his grace given you in Christ Jesus. For in him you have been enriched in every way—in all your speaking and in all your knowledge— because our testimony about Christ was confirmed in you. Therefore you do not lack any spiritual gift as you eagerly wait for our Lord Jesus Christ to be revealed. He will keep you strong to the end, so that you will be blameless on the day of our Lord Jesus Christ.

1 CORINTHIANS 1:4–8 NIV

■ For you are a people holy to the LORD your God. The LORD your God has chosen you out of all the peoples on the face of the earth to be his people, his treasured possession.

DEUTERONOMY 7:6 NIV

■ And God is able to make all grace abound to you, so that in all things at all times, having all that you need, you will abound in every good work.

2 CORINTHIANS 9:8 NIV

■ "Repent, then, and turn to God, so that your sins may be wiped out, that times of refreshing may come from the Lord."

ACTS 3:19 NIV

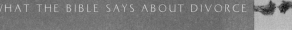

Each of you has been blessed with one of God's many wonderful gifts to be used in the service of others. So use your gift well.

1 Peter 4:10 cev

RESISTING BITTERNESS

▪ Above all else, guard your heart,
    for it is the wellspring of life.

PROVERBS 4:23 NIV

▪ Anyone who claims to be in the light but
hates his brother is still in the darkness.
Whoever loves his brother lives in the light,
and there is nothing in him to make him
stumble. But whoever hates his brother is
in the darkness and walks around in the
darkness; he does not know where he is
going, because the darkness has blinded him.

1 JOHN 2:9–11 NIV

▪ Don't grumble against each other, brothers,
or you will be judged. The Judge is standing at
the door!

JAMES 5:9 NIV

Hatred stirs up strife,
> but love covers all offenses.

PROVERBS 10:12 ESV

People may cover their hatred with pleasant words, but they're deceiving you. They pretend to be kind, but don't believe them. Their hearts are full of many evils. While their hatred may be concealed by trickery, their wrongdoing will be exposed in public.

PROVERBS 26:24–26 NLT

Imitate God, therefore, in everything you do, because you are his dear children. Live a life filled with love, following the example of Christ. He loved us and offered himself as a sacrifice for us, a pleasing aroma to God.

EPHESIANS 5:1–2 NLT

■ Keep a sharp eye out for weeds of bitter discontent. A thistle or two gone to seed can ruin a whole garden in no time.

HEBREWS 12:15 MSG

■ My friends, you were chosen to be free. So don't use your freedom as an excuse to do anything you want. Use it as an opportunity to serve each other with love. All that the Law says can be summed up in the command to love others as much as you love yourself. But if you keep attacking each other like wild animals, you had better watch out or you will destroy yourselves.

GALATIANS 5:13–15 CEV

■ Brothers, if someone is caught in a sin, you who are spiritual should restore him gently. But watch yourself, or you also may be tempted.

GALATIANS 6:1 NIV

DEALING WITH DEPRESSION

■ See how very much our Father loves us,
for he calls us his children, and that is what
we are!

1 JOHN 3:1 NLT

■ "The LORD your God is in your midst,
a mighty one who will save;
he will rejoice over you with gladness;
he will quiet you by his love,
he will exult over you with loud singing."

ZEPHANIAH 3:17 ESV

■ Give thanks in all circumstances, for this is
God's will for you in Christ Jesus.

1 THESSALONIANS 5:18 NIV

■ I waited patiently for the LORD to help me,
    and he turned to me and heard my cry.
He lifted me out of the pit of despair,
    out of the mud and the mire.
He set my feet on solid ground
    and steadied me as I walked along.

PSALM 40:1–2 NLT

■ Don't worry about anything; instead, pray
about everything. Tell God what you need,
and thank him for all he has done. Then you
will experience God's peace, which exceeds
anything we can understand. His peace will
guard your hearts and minds as you live in
Christ Jesus.

PHILIPPIANS 4:6–7 NLT

■ I have received such wonderful revelations
from God. So to keep me from
becoming proud, I was given a thorn in my

flesh, a messenger from Satan to torment me and keep me from becoming proud.

Three different times I begged the Lord to take it away. Each time he said, "My grace is all you need. My power works best in weakness." So now I am glad to boast about my weaknesses, so that the power of Christ can work through me.

2 CORINTHIANS 12:7–9 NLT

"He cuts off every branch in me that bears no fruit, while every branch that does bear fruit he prunes so that it will be even more fruitful."

JOHN 15:2 NIV

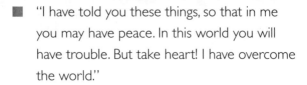
▪ "I have told you these things, so that in me
you may have peace. In this world you will
have trouble. But take heart! I have overcome
the world."

JOHN 16:33 NIV

▪ Yet you brought me out of the womb;
    you made me trust in you
    even at my mother's breast.
From birth I was cast upon you;
    from my mother's womb you have
    been my God.
Do not be far from me,
    for trouble is near
    and there is no one to help.

PSALM 22:9–11 NIV

■ For the creation was subjected to
frustration, not by its own choice, but
by the will of the one who subjected it,
in hope that the creation itself will be
liberated from its bondage to decay and
brought into the glorious freedom of the
children of God.

ROMANS 8:20–21 NIV

■ Yet you are enthroned as the Holy One;
    you are the praise of Israel.
In you our fathers put their trust;
    they trusted and you delivered them.
They cried to you and were saved;
    in you they trusted and were not
    disappointed.

PSALM 22:3–5 NIV

"Ask and it will be given to you; seek and you will find; knock and the door will be opened to you. For everyone who asks receives; he who seeks finds; and to him who knocks, the door will be opened."

MATTHEW 7:7–8 NIV

LETTING GO

■ "Come to me, all you who are weary and
burdened, and I will give you rest."

MATTHEW 11:28 NIV

■ Don't stay far away, LORD!
My strength comes from you, so hurry
and help.
Rescue me from enemy swords and save me
from those dogs. Don't let lions eat me.
You rescued me from the horns of wild bulls.

PSALM 22:19–21 CEV

■ Not that I have already obtained all this, or
have already been made perfect, but I press
on to take hold of that for which Christ Jesus
took hold of me.

PHILIPPIANS 3:12 NIV

Do not be deceived: God cannot be mocked. A man reaps what he sows. The one who sows to please his sinful nature, from that nature will reap destruction; the one who sows to please the Spirit, from the Spirit will reap eternal life.

GALATIANS 6:7–8 NIV

But I tell you to love your enemies and pray for anyone who mistreats you.

MATTHEW 5:44 CEV

"Be still, and know that I am God;
I will be exalted among the nations,
I will be exalted in the earth."

PSALM 46:10 NIV

"Therefore do not worry about tomorrow, for tomorrow will worry about itself. Each day has enough trouble of its own."

MATTHEW 6:34 NIV

ONE MOMENT
AT A TIME

HANDLING TURBULENT EMOTIONS

1. Expect anger. Even an amicable divorce is going to leave you feeling angry at some moments. Divorce can often bring out the worst of each party.

2. Remember there are two sides. While you may be growing angry at your former spouse, don't forget that you have your own weaknesses. The other party needs grace extended just as you do.

3. Choose to forgive. Despite the profound pain and offense received, resist the temptation to hold onto bitterness. While it may take time to dismiss angry feelings, you can ensure those feelings don't affect the way you act or speak to your former spouse.

4. Get supportive help. There is no shame in getting help during this difficult time. Find a supportive friend, pastor, or counselor who can help you work through these natural feelings. Don't let anger or depression become all-consuming without seeking support.

.

CHAPTER 4

AM I ALONE?

After initial news of our separation got around the gossip mill, people generally stopped checking up on me. I find myself home alone most nights. The phone never rings. The e-mail box is empty.

Sometimes I'm tempted to go out and meet someone else—but I know this can't be the right time and that rebound relationships usually end in a second disaster. But I can't stand to be alone.

I need to reach out and get connected with supportive people. I need to get into their lives and I'll need to allow them to get into mine, too.

■ Steve, age 26, Nevada ■

FINDING HEAVENLY COMFORT

The LORD is near to all who call on him,
to all who call on him in truth.

PSALM 145:18 NIV

Come near to God and he will come near
to you.

JAMES 4:8 NIV

I'm still in your presence,
but you've taken my hand.
You wisely and tenderly lead me,
and then you bless me.

PSALM 73:23–24 MSG

■ You notice everything I do and everywhere
I go.

PSALM 139:3 CEV

■ For this is what the high and lofty One says—
        he who lives forever, whose name is holy:
"I live in a high and holy place,
        but also with him who is contrite and
        lowly in spirit, to revive the spirit of the
        lowly and to revive the heart of the
        contrite."

ISAIAH 57:15 NIV

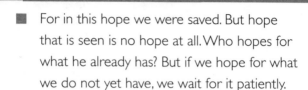
■ For in this hope we were saved. But hope
that is seen is no hope at all. Who hopes for
what he already has? But if we hope for what
we do not yet have, we wait for it patiently.

In the same way, the Spirit helps us in our
weakness. We do not know what we ought
to pray for, but the Spirit himself intercedes
for us with groans that words cannot express.

ROMANS 8:24–26 NIV

■ The beloved of the Lord rests in safety—the
High God surrounds him all day long—
    the beloved rests between his shoulders.

DEUTERONOMY 33:12 NRSV

■ "The young women will dance for joy, and the men—old and young—will join in the celebration. I will turn their mourning into joy. I will comfort them and exchange their sorrow for rejoicing."

JEREMIAH 31:13 NLT

■ "And God will wipe away every tear from their eyes."

REVELATION 7:17 NIV

■ Know therefore that the Lord your God is God; he is the faithful God, keeping his covenant of love to a thousand generations of those who love him and keep his commands.

DEUTERONOMY 7:9 NIV

81

■ Love the LORD your God with all your heart and with all your soul and with all your strength.

DEUTERONOMY 6:5 NIV

■ The LORD your God will be watching to find out whether or not you love him with all your heart and soul.

DEUTERONOMY 13:3 CEV

■ Do not love the world or anything in the world. If anyone loves the world, the love of the Father is not in him.

1 JOHN 2:15 NIV

■ Whom have I in heaven but you?
    And earth has nothing I desire
    besides you.

PSALM 73:25 NIV

■ Delight yourself in the LORD and he will give
you the desires of your heart.

PSALM 37:4 NIV

FINDING EARTHLY SUPPORT

■ Share each other's burdens, and in this way obey the law of Christ.

GALATIANS 6:2 NLT

■ If one part of our body hurts, we hurt all over. If one part of our body is honored, the whole body will be happy.

1 CORINTHIANS 12:26 CEV

■ Be devoted to one another in brotherly love. Honor one another above yourselves.

ROMANS 12:10 NIV

■ Jesus replied: "'Love the Lord your God
with all your heart and with all your soul
and with all your mind.' This is the first and
greatest commandment. And the second is
like it: 'Love your neighbor as yourself.' All the
Law and the Prophets hang on these two
commandments."

MATTHEW 22:37–40 NIV

■ Let's see how inventive we can be in
encouraging love and helping out.

HEBREWS 10:24 MSG

■ There is no fear in love. But perfect love
drives out fear, because fear has to do with
punishment. The one who fears is not made
perfect in love.

1 JOHN 4:18 NIV

■ It's better to have a partner than go it alone.

Share the work, share the wealth.

And if one falls down, the other helps,

But if there's no one to help, tough!

Two in a bed warm each other.

Alone, you shiver all night.

By yourself you're unprotected.

With a friend you can face the worst.

Can you round up a third?

A three-stranded rope isn't easily snapped.

ECCLESIASTES 4:9–12 MSG

LEARNING TO TRUST GOD

■ Though my father and mother forsake me,
the LORD will receive me.

PSALM 27:10 NIV

■ "I will be a Father to you,
and you will be my sons and daughters,
says the Lord Almighty."

2 CORINTHIANS 6:18 NIV

■ God makes homes for the homeless,
leads prisoners to freedom,
but leaves rebels to rot in hell.

PSALM 68:6 MSG

■ "Surely I am with you always, to the very end
of the age."

MATTHEW 28:20 NIV

87

■ "I am with you and will watch over you wherever you go, and I will bring you back to this land. I will not leave you until I have done what I have promised you."

GENESIS 28:15 NIV

■ Those who know your name will trust in you, for you, LORD, have never forsaken those who seek you.

PSALM 9:10 NIV

■ You, LORD, are the light that keeps me safe. I am not afraid of anyone. You protect me, and I have no fears.

PSALM 27:1 CEV

■ Yet I am poor and needy;

may the Lord think of me.

You are my help and my deliverer;

O my God, do not delay.

PSALM 40:17 NIV

■ The steps of a good man are ordered by the
LORD, and He delights in his way.

PSALM 37:23 NKJV

■ Where can I go from your Spirit?

Where can I flee from your presence?

If I go up to the heavens, you are there;

if I make my bed in the depths, you are
there.

If I rise on the wings of the dawn,

if I settle on the far side of the sea,

even there your hand will guide me,

your right hand will hold me fast.

PSALM 139:7–10 NIV

PLUGGING INTO A GOOD CHURCH

■ But God has combined the members of
the body and has given greater honor to
the parts that lacked it, so that there should
be no division in the body, but that its parts
should have equal concern for each other.

1 CORINTHIANS 12:24–25 NIV

■ Now these are the gifts Christ gave to
the church: the apostles, the prophets, the
evangelists, and the pastors and teachers.
Their responsibility is to equip God's people
to do his work and build up the church,
the body of Christ. This will continue until
we all come to such unity in our faith and
knowledge of God's Son that we will be
mature in the Lord, measuring up to the full
and complete standard of Christ.

EPHESIANS 4:11–13 NLT

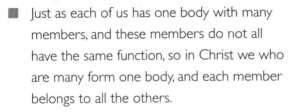

Just as each of us has one body with many members, and these members do not all have the same function, so in Christ we who are many form one body, and each member belongs to all the others.

ROMANS 12:4–5 NIV

Let the peace of Christ rule in your hearts, since as members of one body you were called to peace. And be thankful.

COLOSSIANS 3:15 NIV

Consequently, you are no longer foreigners and aliens, but fellow citizens with God's people and members of God's household. ...

And in him you too are being built together to become a dwelling in which God lives by his Spirit.

EPHESIANS 2:19, 22 NIV

91

■ And you are living stones that God is building
into his spiritual temple. What's more, you
are his holy priests. Through the mediation of
Jesus Christ, you offer spiritual sacrifices that
please God.

1 PETER 2:5 NLT

■ Your kingdom is an everlasting kingdom,
and your dominion endures through
all generations.
The LORD is faithful to all his promises
and loving toward all he has made.

PSALM 145:13 NIV

■ For a day in your courts is better
than a thousand elsewhere.
I would rather be a doorkeeper in the house
of my God than dwell in the tents of
wickedness.

PSALM 84:10 ESV

AVOIDING THE REBOUND

■ A righteous man is cautious in friendship, but
the way of the wicked leads them astray.

PROVERBS 12:26 NIV

■ Let us behave decently, as in the daytime,
not in orgies and drunkenness, not in sexual
immorality and debauchery, not in dissension
and jealousy.

ROMANS 13:13 NIV

■ Those who trust their own insight are foolish,
but anyone who walks in wisdom is safe.

PROVERBS 28:26 NLT

■ Friends come and friends go,
but a true friend sticks by you like family.

PROVERBS 18:24 MSG

ONE MOMENT
AT A TIME

REFUSING TO
BE ALONE

1. Let others love you. Sometimes it can be difficult to let others help you. Accept their love as a mark of friendship and as an example of Christ's love. Don't try to keep track of the good deeds so that you can repay them later.

2. Get involved in a Christ-centered community. God created the church as a place where God's love can be given, received, and shared in practical ways. Churches are made up of struggling people and they exist to provide help as you continue to further your walk with Christ.

3. Avoid the rebound. Rebound relationships can be tempting but almost always deliver additional heartbreak. Have a friend keep you accountable in your relationships with the opposite sex. Now may not be the best time to get involved again. ´

CHAPTER 5

WHERE WILL THE MONEY COME FROM?

I used to be a mom who flagged down the
ice-cream truck and let the kids each grab a
candy from the grocery check-out line.
Now each time I hear the bells of that truck or
see a display of bubble gum, I'm reminded that
I don't even have the money to pay the rent.
I've whittled and whittled the budget, but there's
still not enough to get through the month.

■ Amanda, age 40, California ■

ASKING GOD FOR HELP

■ "For I know the plans I have for you," declares
the LORD, "plans to prosper you and not
to harm you, plans to give you hope and a
future."

JEREMIAH 29:11 NIV

■ "Which of you, if his son asks for bread,
will give him a stone? Or if he asks for a fish,
will give him a snake? If you, then, though
you are evil, know how to give good gifts
to your children, how much more will your
Father in heaven give good gifts to those
who ask him!"

MATTHEW 7:9–11 NIV

All silver and gold belong to me [says the Lord].

HAGGAI 2:8 CEV

The earth is the LORD's, and everything in it, the world, and all who live in it.

PSALM 24:1 NIV

Tell them to have faith in God, who is rich and blesses us with everything we need to enjoy life.

1 TIMOTHY 6:17 CEV

"Until now you have not asked for anything in my name. Ask and you will receive, and your joy will be complete."

JOHN 16:24 NIV

■ And we are confident that he hears us whenever we ask him for anything that pleases him. And since we know he hears us when we make our requests, we also know that he will give us what we ask for.

1 JOHN 5:14–15 NLT

■ You want what you don't have, so you scheme and kill to get it. You are jealous of what others have, but you can't get it, so you fight and wage war to take it away from them. Yet you don't have what you want because you don't ask God for it.

JAMES 4:2 NLT

■ Every good and perfect gift is from above, coming down from the Father of the heavenly lights, who does not change like shifting shadows.

JAMES 1:17 NIV

FINDING GOD'S PROVISION

■ "Don't store up treasures here on earth, where moths eat them and rust destroys them, and where thieves break in and steal. Store your treasures in heaven, where moths and rust cannot destroy, and thieves do not break in and steal. Wherever your treasure is, there the desires of your heart will also be.

"Your eye is a lamp that provides light for your body. When your eye is good, your whole body is filled with light. But when your eye is bad, your whole body is filled with darkness. And if the light you think you have is actually darkness, how deep that darkness is!

"No one can serve two masters. For you will hate one and love the other; you will be devoted to one and despise the other. You cannot serve both God and money.

"That is why I tell you not to worry

about everyday life—whether you have enough food and drink, or enough clothes to wear. Isn't life more than food, and your body more than clothing? Look at the birds. They don't plant or harvest or store food in barns, for your heavenly Father feeds them. And aren't you far more valuable to him than they are? Can all your worries add a single moment to your life?

"And why worry about your clothing? Look at the lilies of the field and how they grow. They don't work or make their clothing, yet Solomon in all his glory was not dressed as beautifully as they are. And if God cares so wonderfully for wildflowers that are here today and thrown into the fire tomorrow, he will certainly care for you. Why do you have so little faith?

"So don't worry about these things, saying, 'What will we eat? What will we drink? What will we wear?' These things dominate the thoughts of unbelievers, but

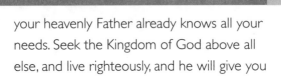

your heavenly Father already knows all your
needs. Seek the Kingdom of God above all
else, and live righteously, and he will give you
everything you need."

MATTHEW 6:19–33 NLT

The Maker of heaven and earth,
      the sea, and everything in them—
      the LORD, who remains faithful forever.
He upholds the cause of the oppressed
      and gives food to the hungry.
The LORD sets prisoners free,
      the LORD gives sight to the blind,
the LORD lifts up those who are bowed down,
      the LORD loves the righteous.
The LORD watches over the alien
      and sustains the fatherless and the widow,
      but he frustrates the ways of the wicked.

PSALM 146:6–9 NIV

■ Do not wear yourself out to get rich;
    have the wisdom to show restraint.
Cast but a glance at riches, and they are gone,
    for they will surely sprout wings
    and fly off to the sky like an eagle.

PROVERBS 23:4–5 NIV

■ Not that I was ever in need, for I have
learned how to be content with whatever I
have. I know how to live on almost nothing
or with everything. I have learned the secret
of living in every situation, whether it is with
a full stomach or empty, with plenty or little.
For I can do everything through Christ, who
gives me strength.

PHILIPPIANS 4:11–13 NLT

BECOMING A GOOD STEWARD

■ "For all the animals of the forest are mine,
    and I own the cattle on a thousand hills.
I know every bird on the mountains,
    and all the animals of the field are mine.
If I were hungry, I would not tell you,
    for all the world is mine and everything
    in it."

PSALM 50:10–12 NLT

■ Everything comes from the Lord. All things were made because of him and will return to him. Praise the Lord forever! Amen.

ROMANS 11:36 CEV

■ God's blessing makes life rich;
nothing we do can improve on God.

PROVERBS 10:22 MSG

■ But remember the LORD your God, for it
is he who gives you the ability to produce
wealth, and so confirms his covenant,
which he swore to your forefathers,
as it is today.

DEUTERONOMY 8:18 NIV

■ Moreover, it is required of stewards that they
be found trustworthy.

1 CORINTHIANS 4:2 ESV

■ "From everyone who has been given much, much will be demanded; and from the one who has been entrusted with much, much more will be asked."

LUKE 12:48 NIV

ONE MOMENT
AT A TIME

LOOKING
TO GOD

■ 1. Define your needs. Make a list of the things you need to live. Try to separate things that you'd like to have from things you need to have.

■ 2. Spend regular time in prayer. God loves you very much. Tell Him about the needs you have.

■ 3. Make necessary changes. Divorce often changes immediate living or buying habits. Consider big changes such as moving to a smaller, more affordable home. Be strong in little changes such as resisting impulse items at the store.

4. Allow others to help. It can be difficult to let others know about your needs, but by doing so you may find that there are friends, family members, or people at church who want to help you with no expectation of anything in return.

CHAPTER 6

HOW WILL THIS AFFECT MY KIDS?

Many nights I lie awake and wonder how I'm going to make it through this. More than that, I worry about how my kids are handling the divorce. I worry that they might feel like it's their fault or that I've totally messed up their lives. While I had some choice in this, they're being unfairly pulled along. I can't help but want to vent at the kids, but I know it's not fair to put them in the middle like that. I just don't know how to help them through this.

■ Beth, age 40, South Carolina ■

MINIMIZING THEIR GUILT

■ But Jesus said, "Let the little children come to me and do not hinder them, for to such belongs the kingdom of heaven."

MATTHEW 19:14 ESV

■ He comforts us in all our troubles so that we can comfort others. When they are troubled, we will be able to give them the same comfort God has given us.

2 CORINTHIANS 1:4 NLT

■ God is our refuge and strength,
    always ready to help in times of trouble.

PSALM 46:1 NLT

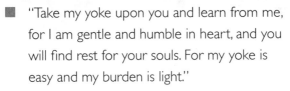

■ "Take my yoke upon you and learn from me, for I am gentle and humble in heart, and you will find rest for your souls. For my yoke is easy and my burden is light."

MATTHEW 11:29–30 NIV

■ LORD, if you kept a record of our sins,
   who, O Lord, could ever survive?
But you offer forgiveness,
   that we might learn to fear you.

PSALM 130:3–4 NLT

■ Have mercy on me, O God, have mercy on me,
   for in you my soul takes refuge.
   I will take refuge in the shadow of your
   wings until the disaster has passed.

PSALM 57:1 NIV

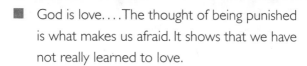

God is love. . . . The thought of being punished is what makes us afraid. It shows that we have not really learned to love.

1 JOHN 4:16, 18 CEV

I am surrounded by trouble,
      but you protect me
      against my angry enemies.
With your own powerful arm
      you keep me safe.

PSALM 138:7 CEV

HELPING THEM HEAL

■ Stoop down and reach out to those who are oppressed. Share their burdens, and so complete Christ's law.

GALATIANS 6:2 MSG

■ Be brave and strong! Don't be afraid. . .The LORD your God will always be at your side, and he will never abandon you.

DEUTERONOMY 31:6 CEV

■ "Have I not commanded you? Be strong and courageous. Do not be terrified; do not be discouraged, for the LORD your God will be with you wherever you go."

JOSHUA 1:9 NIV

"Peace I leave with you; my peace I give to you. Not as the world gives do I give to you. Let not your hearts be troubled, neither let them be afraid."

JOHN 14:27 ESV

CARRYING YOUR OWN BURDENS

■ Fathers, do not embitter your children, or they will become discouraged.

COLOSSIANS 3:21 NIV

■ I look up to the mountains; does my strength come from mountains?
No, my strength comes from God, who made heaven, and earth, and mountains.

PSALM 121:1–2 MSG

■ Don't be afraid. I am with you.
Don't tremble with fear.
I am your God.
I will make you strong,
as I protect you with my arm
and give you victories.

ISAIAH 41:10 CEV

■ "I, your God,
    have a firm grip on you and I'm not
    letting go.
I'm telling you, 'Don't panic.
    I'm right here to help you.' "

ISAIAH 41:13 MSG

■ "Be fair to the poor
and to orphans.
Defend the helpless
and everyone in need."

PSALM 82:3–4 CEV

AVOIDING A TOXIC RELATIONSHIP WITH YOUR EX

■ My dear friends, we must love each other. Love comes from God, and when we love each other, it shows that we have been given new life. We are now God's children, and we know him.

1 JOHN 4:7 CEV

■ If you churn milk
you get butter;
if you pound on your nose,
you get blood—
and if you stay angry,
you get in trouble.

PROVERBS 30:33 CEV

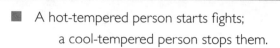

■ A hot-tempered person starts fights;
   a cool-tempered person stops them.

PROVERBS 15:18 NLT

■ Fools show their anger at once,
   but the prudent ignore an insult.

PROVERBS 12:16 NRSV

■ Greed causes fighting;
   trusting the LORD leads to prosperity.

PROVERBS 28:25 NLT

■ Do not gloat when your enemy falls;
   when he stumbles, do not let your heart
   rejoice, or the LORD will see and disapprove.

PROVERBS 24:17–18 NIV

■ Work at living in peace with everyone, and work at living a holy life, for those who are not holy will not see the Lord.

HEBREWS 12:14 NLT

■ Therefore let us pursue the things which make for peace and the things by which one may edify another.

ROMANS 14:19 NKJV

ONE MOMENT
AT A TIME

HELPING YOUR
KIDS ENDURE
DIVORCE

1. Keep the peace. No matter the differences you face and the injustices you feel, your kids need you to handle this situation civilly. While you may not feel like offering Christian love and kindness to your ex, your kids need you to.

2. Don't put them in the middle. Don't let your children become pawns in the disagreements. The differences you face with your ex are yours, not theirs. It's almost never appropriate to vent to them about

the frustrations you feel about your ex. Don't force your kids to take sides.

3. Work it out. Parents need to be at ballgames, recitals, and concerts. Don't let bickering with a spouse keep you away from supporting your kids and showing the love they need.

4. Find some support. You're not the only person in this who needs a friend and listening ear. Let your kids visit with friends and their families, travel to see Grandma, and consider a professional counselor to help them work through their own issues.

CHAPTER 7

WILL I ALWAYS BE THIS EXHAUSTED?

Every afternoon it's the same: I drive from ballet to baseball to scouts and finally find my way home. I put the kids to bed and get caught up on the office work that I bring home. Usually after midnight, I'm able to haul myself to bed. The morning begins again with the relentless routine of getting the kids off to school and myself to work. Once the workday ends, the afternoon merry-go-round begins again. I've been working on five hours of sleep for too long. I'm not sure how much longer I'll be able to make it.

■ Ben, age 34, Illinois ■

FINDING PHYSICAL REST

 Do you not know?
>   Have you not heard?
> The LORD is the everlasting God,
>   the Creator of the ends of the earth.
> He will not grow tired or weary,
>   and his understanding no one
>   can fathom.
> He gives strength to the weary
>   and increases the power of the weak.
> Even youths grow tired and weary,
>   and young men stumble and fall;
> but those who hope in the LORD
>   will renew their strength.
> They will soar on wings like eagles;
>   they will run and not grow weary,
>   they will walk and not be faint.

ISAIAH 40:28–31 NIV

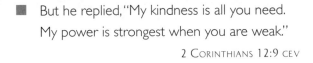

■ But he replied, "My kindness is all you need.
My power is strongest when you are weak."

2 CORINTHIANS 12:9 CEV

■ Though an army besiege me,
    my heart will not fear;
though war break out against me,
    even then will I be confident.

PSALM 27:3 NIV

■ "The eternal God is your refuge,
    and underneath are the everlasting arms."

DEUTERONOMY 33:27 NIV

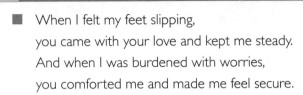
■ When I felt my feet slipping,
   you came with your love and kept me steady.
   And when I was burdened with worries,
   you comforted me and made me feel secure.

PSALM 94:18–19 CEV

BEING STILL FOR A MOMENT

■ "Be still, and know that I am God;
    I will be exalted among the nations,
    I will be exalted in the earth."

PSALM 46:10 NIV

■ The LORD replied, "My Presence will go with you, and I will give you rest."

EXODUS 33:14 NIV

■ Cast all your anxiety on him because he cares for you.

1 PETER 5:7 NIV

■ Showing respect to the LORD brings true life—if you do it, you can relax without fear of danger.

PROVERBS 19:23 CEV

■ "You keep him in perfect peace
   whose mind is stayed on you,
   because he trusts in you.
Trust in the LORD forever,
   for the LORD GOD is an everlasting rock.

ISAIAH 26:3–4 ESV

■ "Can all your worries add a single moment to your life? And if worry can't accomplish a little thing like that, what's the use of worrying over bigger things?"

LUKE 12:25–26 NLT

■ I sought the LORD, and he answered me;
    he delivered me from all my fears.

PSALM 34:4 NIV

■ Think about the things of heaven, not the
things of earth. For you died to this life, and
your real life is hidden with Christ in God. And
when Christ, who is your life, is revealed to the
whole world, you will share in all his glory.

COLOSSIANS 3:2–4 NLT

REFRESHING YOUR HEART

The LORD is near to all who call on him,
   to all who call on him in truth.
He fulfills the desires of those who fear him;
   he hears their cry and saves them.

PSALM 145:18–19 NIV

When I called, you answered me;
   you made me bold and stouthearted.

PSALM 138:3 NIV

Search me, O God, and know my heart;
   test me and know my anxious thoughts.

PSALM 139:23 NLT

■ Let me abide in your tent forever,
    find refuge under the shelter of your
    wings.

PSALM 61:4 NRSV

■ Let all bitterness and wrath and anger and
clamor and slander be put away from you,
along with all malice.

EPHESIANS 4:31 ESV

Wait for the LORD;
    be strong and take heart
    and wait for the LORD.

PSALM 27:14 NIV

ONE MOMENT
AT A TIME

FEELING
MAXED OUT?

■ 1. Look for changes. Make a list of the activities that exhaust you. While you may prefer to leave your routine alone, are you able to make some changes—even temporarily—to help ease the stress?

■ 2. Be realistic. You can't work ninety hours a week, be a full-time parent, coach your kid's team, and find time to sing in the church choir. Prioritize what you can do and choose to feel good about the things God has allowed you to do.

■ 3. Don't forget God. As you grow busy and

tired, it may become easy for you to reduce your regular time spent with God. Don't do it. Your dependency on God is more vital now than ever.

4. Do something for yourself. Find some time each week to take a genuine break. It can be some quiet moments in the car or a few extra minutes in the shower. Do your best to push the busy and exhausting thoughts from your mind and just enjoy the quiet.

CHAPTER 8

WHAT ABOUT SEX?

I miss sex. I know that sounds crazy to some women, but I really miss the physical and emotional intimacy. Sometimes the tempting thoughts come while I'm with a coworker or even sometimes when I'm at church. There are a couple of men at each place who flirt with me and I think they may be interested. Sometimes I'm tempted to think, What would be the harm?

■ Jocelyn, age 39, Washington, DC ■

PRESERVING PURITY

■ Instead, clothe yourself with the presence of
the Lord Jesus Christ. And don't let yourself
think about ways to indulge your evil desires.

ROMANS 13:14 NLT

■ Run from anything that stimulates youthful
lusts. Instead, pursue righteous living,
faithfulness, love, and peace. Enjoy the
companionship of those who call on the
Lord with pure hearts.

2 TIMOTHY 2:22 NLT

■ The acts of the sinful nature are obvious:
sexual immorality, impurity and debauchery.

GALATIANS 5:19 NIV

■ Put to death, therefore, whatever belongs to your earthly nature: sexual immorality, impurity, lust, evil desires and greed, which is idolatry.

COLOSSIANS 3:5 NIV

■ Or do you not know that your body is the temple of the Holy Spirit who is in you, whom you have from God, and you are not your own? For you were bought at a price; therefore glorify God in your body and in your spirit, which are God's.

1 CORINTHIANS 6:19–20 NKJV

■ But now you must be holy in everything you do, just as God who chose you is holy. For said the Scriptures say, "You must be holy because I am holy."

1 PETER 1:15–16 NLT

▪ God's will is for you to be holy, so stay away from all sexual sin.

1 THESSALONIANS 4:3 NLT

▪ "But I tell you that anyone who looks at a woman lustfully has already committed adultery with her in his heart."

MATTHEW 5:28 NIV

▪ But each person is tempted when he is lured and enticed by his own desire.

JAMES 1:14 ESV

▪ Honor marriage, and guard the sacredness of sexual intimacy between wife and husband. God draws a firm line against casual and illicit sex.

HEBREWS 13:4 MSG

AVOIDING TEMPTATION

■ Be self-controlled and alert. Your enemy the devil prowls around like a roaring lion looking for someone to devour. Resist him, standing firm in the faith, because you know that your brothers throughout the world are undergoing the same kind of sufferings.

And the God of all grace, who called you to his eternal glory in Christ, after you have suffered a little while, will himself restore you and make you strong, firm and steadfast.

1 PETER 5:8–10 NIV

■ So humble yourselves before God. Resist the devil, and he will flee from you.

JAMES 4:7 NLT

141

■ The temptations in your life are no different from what others experience. And God is faithful. He will not allow the temptation to be more than you can stand. When you are tempted, he will show you a way out so that you can endure.

1 CORINTHIANS 10:13 NLT

■ God blesses those who patiently endure testing and temptation. Afterward they will receive the crown of life that God has promised to those who love him. And remember, when you are being tempted, do not say, "God is tempting me." God is never tempted to do wrong, and he never tempts anyone else.

JAMES 1:12–13 NLT

■ For we do not have a high priest who is
unable to sympathize with our weaknesses,
but we have one who has been tempted in
every way, just as we are—yet was without
sin. Let us then approach the throne of grace
with confidence, so that we may receive
mercy and find grace to help us in our time
of need.

HEBREWS 4:15–16 NIV

■ How can a young person stay pure?
    By obeying your word.
I have tried hard to find you—
    don't let me wander from your commands.
I have hidden your word in my heart,
    that I might not sin against you.

PSALM 119:9–11 NLT

KNOWING YOUR LIMITATIONS

Finally, brothers, whatever is true, whatever is noble, whatever is right, whatever is pure, whatever is lovely, whatever is admirable—if anything is excellent or praiseworthy—think about such things.

PHILIPPIANS 4:8 NIV

But among you there must not be even a hint of sexual immorality, or of any kind of impurity, or of greed, because these are improper for God's holy people.

EPHESIANS 5:3 NIV

So let us not grow weary in doing what is right, for we will reap at harvest time, if we do not give up.

GALATIANS 6:9 NRSV

■ Those who live according to the sinful nature have their minds set on what that nature desires; but those who live in accordance with the Spirit have their minds set on what the Spirit desires.

ROMANS 8:5 NIV

■ With all your heart you must trust the LORD and not your own judgment.

Always let him lead you, and he will clear the road for you to follow.

PROVERBS 3:5–6 CEV

■ For the grace of God that brings salvation has appeared to all men. It teaches us to say "No" to ungodliness and worldly passions, and to live self-controlled, upright and godly lives in this present age.

TITUS 2:11–12 NIV

■ As obedient children, do not conform to the evil desires you had when you lived in ignorance.

1 PETER 1:14 NIV

■ Don't be selfish; don't try to impress others. Be humble, thinking of others as better than yourselves. Don't look out only for your own interests, but take an interest in others, too.

PHILIPPIANS 2:3–4 NLT

■ Train me in good common sense;
I'm thoroughly committed to living your way.

PSALM 119:66 MSG

■ I will instruct you and teach you in the way you should go;
I will counsel you and watch over you.

PSALM 32:8 NIV

■ Put on all the armor that God gives, so you can defend yourself against the devil's tricks.

EPHESIANS 6:11 CEV

■ For this reason, since the day we heard about you, we have not stopped praying for you and asking God to fill you with the knowledge of his will through all spiritual wisdom and understanding. And we pray this in order that you may live a life worthy of the Lord and may please him in every way: bearing fruit in every good work, growing in the knowledge of God, being strengthened with all power according to his glorious might so that you may have great endurance and patience, and joyfully giving thanks to the Father, who has qualified you to share in the inheritance of the saints in the kingdom of light.

COLOSSIANS 1:9–12 NIV

ACKNOWLEDGING YOUR NEED FOR INTIMACY

■ The Lord God said,

"It is not good for the man to be alone.
I will make a helper suitable for him."

So the Lord God caused the man to fall
into a deep sleep; and while he was sleeping,
he took one of the man's ribs and closed
up the place with flesh. Then the Lord God
made a woman from the rib he had taken
out of the man, and he brought her to
the man.

The man said,

"This is now bone of my bones
and flesh of my flesh;
she shall be called 'woman,'
for she was taken out of man."

For this reason a man will leave his father
and mother and be united to his wife, and
they will become one flesh.

Genesis 2:18, 21–24 niv

■ Wise friends make you wise,
   but you hurt yourself by going around
   with fools.

PROVERBS 13:20 CEV

■ Don't fool yourselves. Bad friends will
   destroy you.

1 CORINTHIANS 15:33 CEV

■ Stay away from fools, for you won't find
   knowledge on their lips.

PROVERBS 14:7 NLT

■ You can trust a friend who corrects you,
   but kisses from an enemy are nothing
   but lies.

PROVERBS 27:6 CEV

ONE MOMENT
AT A TIME

ESTABLISHING
BOUNDARIES

■ 1. Remember God's standards. While our society has redefined and accepted casual sex, God's standards haven't changed. Keep your heart focused on Christ.

■ 2. Acknowledge your need for intimacy. God created you with a desire for intimacy. Realize that need is natural, then spend your efforts deepening your relationship with Him and with friends of the same sex.

■ 3. Know your limitations. If certain magazines, books, or movies feed your sexual desires, then put them aside. If you find that certain people in your life invite temptation, then change the way you interact with them. Have a friend of the same sex hold you accountable to God's standards.

■ 4. Be honest with yourself. Sexual temptation is easy to enjoy. Recognize when you find yourself lingering on thoughts or images you should dismiss and then move quickly to do so.

CHAPTER 9

DO I HAVE TO FORGIVE?

I'm so hurt and angry that I find myself lashing out in ways I didn't think were possible for me. My ex-husband and I can't be in the same room without one or both of us screaming at the other. We've tried to discuss our differences over the phone, but we can't last more than two minutes without one of us hanging up on the other. Now we do all of our talking through lawyers.

■ Becca, age 52, Colorado ■

FORGIVING YOUR EX

■ Be kind and compassionate to one another,
forgiving each other, just as in Christ God
forgave you.

EPHESIANS 4:32 NIV

■ The Lord passed before him, and proclaimed,
"The Lord, the Lord, a God merciful and
gracious, slow to anger, and abounding in
steadfast love and faithfulness."

EXODUS 34:6 NRSV

■ Dear friends, let us continue to love one
another, for love comes from God. Anyone
who loves is a child of God and knows God.
But anyone who does not love does not
know God—for God is love.

1 JOHN 4:7–8 NLT

"But love your enemies, do good to them, and lend to them without expecting to get anything back. Then your reward will be great, and you will be sons of the Most High, because he is kind to the ungrateful and wicked. Be merciful, just as your Father is merciful.

Do not judge, and you will not be judged. Do not condemn, and you will not be condemned. Forgive, and you will be forgiven. Give, and it will be given to you. A good measure, pressed down, shaken together and running over, will be poured into your lap. For with the measure you use, it will be measured to you."

LUKE 6:35–38 NIV

He who covers a transgression seeks love,
But he who repeats a matter separates
    friends.

PROVERBS 17:9 NKJV

■ Then Peter came to Jesus and asked, "Lord, how many times shall I forgive my brother when he sins against me? Up to seven times?"

Jesus answered, "I tell you, not seven times, but seventy-seven times."

MATTHEW 18:21–22 NIV

■ "So watch yourselves! If another believer sins, rebuke that person; then if there is repentance, forgive. Even if that person wrongs you seven times a day and each time turns again and asks forgiveness, you must forgive."

LUKE 17:3–4 NLT

■ But when you are praying, first forgive anyone you are holding a grudge against, so that your Father in heaven will forgive your sins, too.

MARK 11:25 NLT

DEALING WITH ADVERSARIAL PEOPLE

■ Only fools get angry quickly and hold a grudge.

ECCLESIASTES 7:9 CEV

■ Do not let any unwholesome talk come out of your mouths, but only what is helpful for building others up according to their needs, that it may benefit those who listen.

EPHESIANS 4:29 NIV

■ Never pay back evil with more evil. Do things in such a way that everyone can see you are honorable. Do all that you can to live in peace with everyone.

ROMANS 12:17–18 NLT

■ Short-tempered people do foolish things, and schemers are hated.

PROVERBS 14:17 NLT

■ "You shall not hate your brother in your heart, but you shall reason frankly with your neighbor, lest you incur sin because of him. You shall not take vengeance or bear a grudge against the sons of your own people, but you shall love your neighbor as yourself: I am the LORD."

LEVITICUS 19:17–18 ESV

■ Quick, GOD, I need your helping hand!
The last decent person just went down,
All the friends I depended on gone.

PSALM 12:1 MSG

■ One who is slow to anger is better than the mighty, and one whose temper is controlled than one who captures a city.

PROVERBS 16:32 NRSV

HANDLING WELL-MEANING BUT INSENSITIVE PEOPLE

■ A gentle answer turns away wrath,

but a harsh word stirs up anger.

PROVERBS 15:1 NIV

■ My dear friends, you should be quick to listen and slow to speak or to get angry.

JAMES 1:19 CEV

■ "Do not judge others, and you will not be judged. For you will be treated as you treat others. The standard you use in judging is the standard by which you will be judged. And why worry about a speck in your friend's eye when you have a log in your own? How can you think of saying to your friend, 'Let me help you get rid of that speck in your eye,'

159

when you can't see past the log in your own eye? Hypocrite! First get rid of the log in your own eye; then you will see well enough to deal with the speck in your friend's eye."

MATTHEW 7:1–5 NLT

"Blessed are those who are persecuted because of righteousness, for theirs is the kingdom of heaven.

"Blessed are you when people insult you, persecute you and falsely say all kinds of evil against you because of me. Rejoice and be glad, because great is your reward in heaven, for in the same way they persecuted the prophets who were before you."

MATTHEW 5:10–12 NIV

■ "For if you forgive others their trespasses,
your heavenly Father will also forgive you."

MATTHEW 6:14 ESV

■ Sensible people control their temper;
they earn respect by overlooking wrongs.

PROVERBS 19:11 NLT

ONE MOMENT
AT A TIME

EXTENDING
FORGIVENESS

1. Focus on the true victim. If you refuse to forgive someone, the person who suffers is you. You're the one who lives with the regular reminders of the pain.

2. Make a list. It's important to realize why you are angry so you can fully forgive and move past the situation. Make a list of things that have bothered you. Then burn the paper or throw the list away. Ask God to help you move past the hurts, too.

3. Understand forgiveness. Forgiveness is choosing to act toward someone as if the

offense did not occur. While hurt feelings may take time to dissipate, your words and actions toward that individual can change today.

4. Seek God's help. True forgiveness may be bigger than what you can accomplish on your own. Spend time with God, asking Him to show you the depth of His forgiveness. Ask for His help in forgiving the people you need to extend similar grace to.

CHAPTER 10

IS RECONCILIATION POSSIBLE?

The ink was hardly dry on our divorce
documents when my ex-husband started saying
that he wanted to reconcile. I don't know if
his motivation is guilt, money, sex, or power.
Whatever it is, the thought of getting back
together scares me. I know God hates divorce,
but I can't take my kids and go back into a bad
situation. While divorce hasn't been a good
option, it's better than living with the verbal
abuse he often heaped on us. And while
he's promised to change, I don't see enough
evidence yet that he really has.

■ Joanna, age 37, New Hampshire ■

BEING OPEN TO RECONCILIATION

■ Love is patient, love is kind. It does not envy, it does not boast, it is not proud. It is not rude, it is not self-seeking, it is not easily angered, it keeps no record of wrongs. Love does not delight in evil but rejoices with the truth. It always protects, always trusts, always hopes, always perseveres.

Love never fails.

1 CORINTHIANS 13:4–8 NIV

■ Always be humble and gentle. Patiently put up with each other and love each other.

EPHESIANS 4:2 CEV

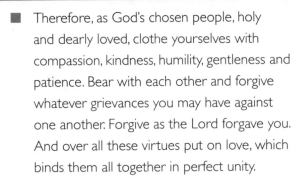

■ Therefore, as God's chosen people, holy and dearly loved, clothe yourselves with compassion, kindness, humility, gentleness and patience. Bear with each other and forgive whatever grievances you may have against one another. Forgive as the Lord forgave you. And over all these virtues put on love, which binds them all together in perfect unity.

COLOSSIANS 3:12–14 NIV

■ So husbands ought to love their own wives as their own bodies; he who loves his wife loves himself. For no one ever hated his own flesh, but nourishes and cherishes it, just as the Lord does the church. For we are members of His body, of His flesh and of His bones. "For this reason a man shall leave his father and mother and be joined to his wife, and the two shall become one flesh."

EPHESIANS 5:28–31 NJKV

PURSUING RECONCILIATION

■ Most important of all, you must sincerely love each other, because love wipes away many sins.

1 PETER 4:8 CEV

■ Therefore, as we have opportunity, let us do good to all people, especially to those who belong to the family of believers.

GALATIANS 6:10 NIV

■ Reckless words pierce like a sword,
    but the tongue of the wise brings healing.

PROVERBS 12:18 NIV

■ "Now that I, your Lord and Teacher, have washed your feet, you also should wash one another's feet. I have set you an example that you should do as I have done for you."

JOHN 13:14–15 NIV

■ "A new command I give you: Love one another. As I have loved you, so you must love one another."

JOHN 13:34 NIV

■ Don't just pretend to love others. Really love them. Hate what is wrong. Hold tightly to what is good. Love each other with genuine affection, and take delight in honoring each other.

ROMANS 12:9–10 NLT

169

■ Husbands, love your wives and do not be harsh with them.

COLOSSIANS 3:19 NIV

■ Do two people walk hand in hand
if they aren't going to the same place?

AMOS 3:3 MSG

■ Finishing is better than starting. Patience is better than pride.

ECCLESIASTES 7:8 NLT

SEEKING WISDOM

■ Search for wisdom as you would search for silver or hidden treasure.

> PROVERBS 2:4 CEV

■ It's much better to be wise and sensible than to be rich.

> PROVERBS 16:16 CEV

■ "First seek the counsel of the LORD."

> 1 KINGS 22:5 NIV

■ Fools think their own way is right, but the wise listen to others.

> PROVERBS 12:15 NLT

■ Listen to advice and accept instruction, and in the end you will be wise.

> PROVERBS 19:20 NIV

ONE MOMENT
AT A TIME

CONSIDERING RECONCILIATION

■ 1. Get good counsel. It's easy to find a friend who will tell you what you want to hear or who will push an agenda (either reconciliation or staying apart). Find a friend, counselor, or pastor who can be objective and help you evaluate your unique situation.

■ 2. Don't rush. While you may feel pressure to make a quick decision, don't act impulsively. Time apart can help determine true motivations as well as provide you the chance to see if the problems that caused the divorce in the first place are still present.

3. Be objective. Don't let wishful thinking or swinging emotions drive you to make a decision you'll regret.

4. Work together. If both parties want reconciliation, then work together in that process. Undergo counseling together before taking big steps to ensure you will be able to live together again under one roof.

CHAPTER 11
CAN I REBUILD MY LIFE?

It's been two years since I first heard the words
"I want a divorce." My now ex-husband has
already remarried and has taken a job in another
city. As for me, I struggle to keep the kids
(and our lives) together. While it's been difficult,
I've sensed God's presence during this time.
He's helped me get through the pain and given
me perspective on myself and the future.

■ Cyndi, age 28, Texas ■

DEALING WITH LINGERING HURTS

■ I'll never forget the trouble, the utter lostness,
the taste of ashes, the poison I've
swallowed.
I remember it all—oh, how well I
remember—the feeling of hitting the
bottom.
But there's one other thing I remember,
and remembering, I keep a grip
on hope:
God's loyal love couldn't have run out,
his merciful love couldn't have
dried up.

LAMENTATIONS 3:19–22 MSG

Bring joy to your servant,
    For to you, O Lord,
        I lift up my soul.

PSALM 86:4 NIV

Pray that our LORD
will make us strong and give us peace.

PSALM 29:11 CEV

Praise be to the God and Father of our Lord
Jesus Christ, the Father of compassion and
the God of all comfort.

2 CORINTHIANS 1:3 NIV

For he has not ignored or belittled the
suffering of the needy.
        He has not turned his back on them,
        but has listened to their cries for help.

PSALM 22:24 NLT

I learned God-worship
   when my pride was shattered.
Heart-shattered lives ready for love
   don't for a moment escape God's notice.

PSALM 51:17 MSG

FINDING NEW HOPE

■ Being confident of this, that he who began
a good work in you will carry it on to
completion until the day of Christ Jesus.

PHILIPPIANS 1:6 NIV

■ But you, O Sovereign LORD,
    deal well with me for your name's sake;
    out of the goodness of your love,
    deliver me.
For I am poor and needy,
    and my heart is wounded within me.

PSALM 109:21–22 NIV

■ For you have been my hope, O Sovereign
LORD, my confidence since my youth.

PSALM 71:5 NIV

■ To all who mourn in Israel, he will give a crown of beauty for ashes, a joyous blessing instead of mourning, festive praise instead of despair. In their righteousness, they will be like great oaks that the LORD has planted for his own glory.

ISAIAH 61:3 NLT

I am still confident of this:
　　I will see the goodness of the LORD
　　in the land of the living.
Wait for the LORD;
　　be strong and take heart
　　and wait for the LORD.

PSALM 27:13–14 NIV

■ Why am I discouraged?
Why am I restless? I trust you!
And I will praise you again
     because you help me.

PSALM 42:5 CEV

■ And this same God who takes care of me
will supply all your needs from his glorious
riches, which have been given to us in Christ
Jesus.

PHILIPPIANS 4:19 NLT

■ Trust in the LORD and do good.
Then you will live safely in the land and
     prosper.

PSALM 37:3 NLT

■ Praise the LORD! Oh give thanks to the LORD, for he is good, for his steadfast love endures forever!

PSALM 106:1 ESV

■ Consider it pure joy, my brothers, whenever you face trials of many kinds, because you know that the testing of your faith develops perseverance. Perseverance must finish its work so that you may be mature and complete, not lacking anything.

JAMES 1:2–4 NIV

BELIEVING YOUR SELF-WORTH

■ I praise you because I am fearfully and
wonderfully made;
    your works are wonderful,
    I know that full well.

PSALM 139:14 NIV

■ "Before I shaped you in the womb,
    I knew all about you.
Before you saw the light of day,
    I had holy plans for you."

JEREMIAH 1:5 MSG

■ How far has the LORD taken our sins from us?
Farther than the distance from east to west!

PSALM 103:12 CEV

183

■ How great is the love the Father has lavished
on us, that we should be called children of
God! And that is what we are! The reason
the world does not know us is that it did not
know him.

1 JOHN 3:1 NIV

■ But thanks be to God! He gives us the
victory through our Lord Jesus Christ.

1 CORINTHIANS 15:57 NIV

■ How precious are your thoughts about me,
    O God.
They cannot be numbered!
I can't even count them;
    they outnumber the grains of sand!
And when I wake up,
    you are still with me!

PSALM 139:17–18 NLT

■ Therefore, if anyone is in Christ, he is a new creation; the old has gone, the new has come!

2 CORINTHIANS 5:17 NIV

■ He gave his life to free us from every kind of sin, to cleanse us, and to make us his very own people, totally committed to doing good deeds.

TITUS 2:14 NLT

HEALING THE HEARTBREAK

■ So we can say with confidence,
"The LORD is my helper,
    so I will have no fear.
What can mere people do to me?"

HEBREWS 13:6 NLT

■ The LORD will lead you into the land. He will always be with you and help you, so don't ever be afraid of your enemies.

DEUTERONOMY 31:8 CEV

■ The LORD is my rock, my fortress and my deliverer; my God is my rock, in whom I take refuge. He is my shield and the horn of my salvation, my stronghold.

PSALM 18:2 NIV

■ For he will command his angels concerning
you to guard you in all your ways.

PSALM 91:11 NIV

■ You are my hiding place;
you will protect me from trouble
and surround me with songs of
deliverance.

PSALM 32:7 NIV

■ "When you pass through the waters,
I will be with you;
And through the rivers, they shall not
overflow you.
When you walk through the fire, you shall
not be burned,
Nor shall the flame scorch you."

ISAIAH 43:2 NKJV

Though you have made me see troubles,
many and bitter, you will restore my life again;
from the depths of the earth you will again
bring me up.

PSALM 71:20 NIV

These hard times are small potatoes
compared to the coming good times, the
lavish celebration prepared for us.

2 CORINTHIANS 4:17 MSG

Therefore we will not fear, though the earth
give way and the mountains fall into the
heart of the sea, though its waters roar and
foam and the mountains quake with their
surging.

PSALM 46:2–3 NIV

■ You don't need to cry anymore. The Lord is
kind, and as soon as he hears your cries for
help, he will come.

ISAIAH 30:19 CEV

ONE MOMENT
AT A TIME

PUTTING THE PIECES BACK TOGETHER

1. Recall God's purpose for your life. Remember that God created you intentionally. Part of that purpose is to praise Him; part of that purpose may be to raise the children He's given you. What else has God empowered you to do?

2. Have patience. Divorce takes a lot out of you physically, emotionally, socially, and financially. Don't expect to walk out of divorce court with a sense of closure. It takes most people a couple of years to get past the

hurt and get back on their feet. Be patient with yourself and allow yourself the time you need.

3. Refuse to remain discouraged. Lingering in a state of discouragement is a choice. When those thoughts arise, put them aside and thank God for the blessings He's brought you. In place of feeling defeated, get involved with Christian friends who can direct you closer to Christ. Let good friends help you cultivate your dreams and take next steps in meeting them.

4. Consider your children. While it may be tempting to jump back into a dating relationship or to venture off in a new career, remember that if you have children, you can't make these decisions without consequences. Children need stability and safety. Be sure to consider them in your decision-making process.

Look for all the
What the Bible Says About…
books from Barbour Publishing

What the Bible Says about
GRIEVING
ISBN 978-1-59789-994-9

What the Bible Says about
MARRIAGE
ISBN 978-1-59789-993-2

What the Bible Says about
MONEY
ISBN 978-1-59789-992-5

192 pages / 3 ¾" x 6" / $4.97 each

Available wherever Christian books are sold.